The Jovial Sailor pub on the left at 10.00am on 6 December 2015. **Inset:** a similar view taken on 8 January 2005.

The flooded front entrance of McVities at 10.30 am on 6 December 2015. **Inset:** the same view at about the same time in January 2005.

Looking along Church Street towards Caldew Bridge shows the extent of the flooding at 10.30am on 6 December 2015.
Inset: a similar view about the same time on 8 January 2005.

Looking along Church street towards the Joiners Arms and the Brewery Residences at 10.30 am.
Inset: On my return at about 2.00pm the level had dropped, unlike the situation in 2005.

Hawick street just after 10.30 am 6 December 2015. The water was not quite as high as in 2005 as shown in the inset picture.

Another view along Hawick Street towards Wigton Road. **Inset:** The sewers here were surcharging into the street.

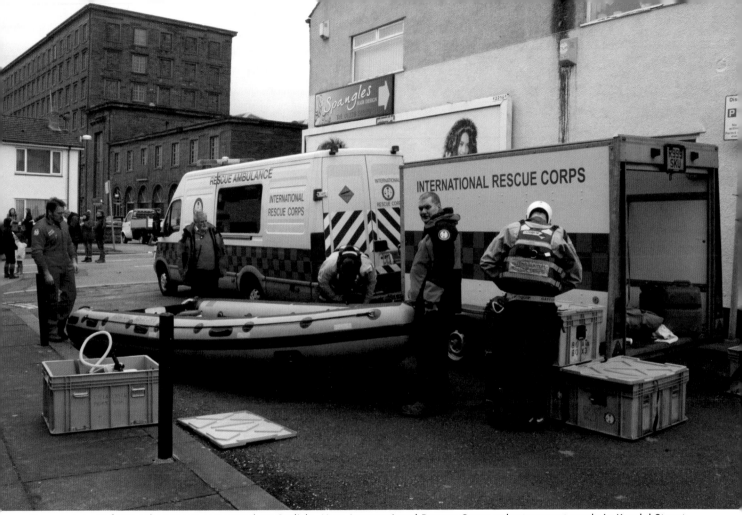

Rescue groups from other areas converged on Carlisle. Here International Rescue Corps volunteers get ready in Kendal Street.

Launching rescue boats in Shaddongate, 2015 at 2.00 pm. **Inset:** Shaddongate In 2005. The water was deeper at this point.

Shaddongate 2.00pm, 2015.

Milbourne Street in 2015. The water is much shallower than in 2005 when it was not possible to enter the street on foot.
Inset: Junction street looking down Charlotte Street to Milbourne Street in 2005.

Inside the image, the newspaper cutting reads:

Party time for flood victims going home

Neighbours out in force to celebrate return to city stree

BY LAURA SHARPE

RESIDENTS of one of Carlisle's worst flood-hit areas are holding a street party today to celebrate moving back home.

More than 140 homes were submerged in four feet of water in January, forcing residents to evacuate their homes.

After an eight month clean-up and rebuild, residents have finally been able to return to their homes and have organised today's event to celebrate.

Weather permitting, tables will be set out in the street and bunting will adorn the houses. If it rains the party will move inside to the Milbourne Arms pub.

Residents of Impact Hous...

Flooded out: Residents of Milbourne Street were forced to throw out most of their property after floods hit Carlisle in January. They are now celebrating their return with a street party

A great community spirit surfaced in Melbourne Street during and after the 2005 floods. See the newspaper cutting from September 2005. On 6 December 2015 tea and coffee were being served by volunteers to other householders in the street.

The Caldew from Nelson bridge in 2015. The viaduct estate on the right was still flooded in spite of the new flood wall.

Viaduct estate near the archway leading to Town Dyke car park and Citadel Station, 6 December 2015.
Inset: The view of the estate from Caldew Bridge in the 2005 floods.

Town Dyke car park below West Walls, Sunday 6 December 2015.

Cars left overnight in Town Dyke car park between West Walls and the West Coast main railway line.

Caldewgate seen from Caldew bridges looking west. The Joiners Arms, centre background, has a plaque recording the 2005 flood level. The picture opposite is a telephoto image of the public house showing that plaque. **Inset:** The same view in 2005.

A telephoto image of the Joiners Arms in 2015. The circular plaque by the door shows the height the flood reached in 2005. In 2015 this height was not reached, probably because of the new flood defences holding back much of the water.

The Caldew spilling over the new defence wall built to protect the Old Brewery residences after 2005.
Inset: A similar view from 2005.

The new wall being overtopped along its length. The Caldew joins the river Eden about half a mile ahead in Bitts Park. This probably caused a backing up of the Caldew's flow causing the river to rise above the height of the defences.

Looking back towards Caldew Bridge. The river at this point has flooded the main railway line.

Occupiers of the Brewery residences observing the river level, seen from Caldew Bridge, 6 December 2015.

Floodwater covers Devonshire Walk car park and the West Coast mainline, seen from the Millennium pedestrian bridge, 2015.

Another view of Devonshire walk car park, with the flooded main railway line and the Brewery residences in the background. The image was taken from the path on the bank below the castle walls.

Bitts Park viewed from the east bank of Carlisle Castle.

Corporation Road at 11.37 am on 6 December 2015.
Inset: Corporation Road at about the same time in January 2005, when the level was lower.

Inset: The same view in 2005.   Castleway looking towards Hardwicke Circus.

A telephoto view from the same position as the image opposite, looking across Hardwicke Circus and the Sands car park to the Turf Inn.

Looking back to Castle Way from the Market Hall, 6 December 2015.

Looking down towards the old fire station, recently converted into a community arts centre.
Inset: A similar picture from the 2005 floods showing people being rescued by boat from Corporation Road.

Carlise Civic Centre from the west end of Drovers Lane in 2015. **Inset:** the same view in 2005.

Carlisle Civic Centre rotunda and the magistrates courts from Drovers' Lane, 6 December 2015.   **Inset:** a similar view in 2005.

Inset: A similar view from 2005, note the flooded cars.   The view from Drovers Lane looking towards the castle, 6 December 2015.

Looking down Georgian Way towards Hardwicke Circus with the Sands Centre and the furniture showroom in the background.
Inset: Further round to the right on the main picture is a DIY store which was closed for many weeks after the 2005 floods.

Strand Road at the junction with Hartington Street in 2015.   **Inset:** the same place in 2005.

Trinity school, suffered worse flooding than in 2005 when only the lower school and sports hall were badly affected.

A closeup of Trinity school which has been largely re-built since the 2005 floods.

Looking down Lismore Place from Victoria Place. Newman School on the right, 6 December 2015.

Inset: Newman School flooded in 2005.

Flooded once more, 6 December 2015.

The grounds to the rear of the Central Academy in Lismore Place, 6 December 2015 at 12.07 pm.

A lot of activity in Broad Street taking sand to fill sandbags. Note the figure in the distance, arrowed.

A telephoto image of the figure in the distance on the previous page.

Inset: a similar image from 2005.　　　Greystone Road, 6 December 2015. Brunton Crescent in the background.

A telephoto image of Brunton Crescent taken from the same place as the image opposite.

Melbourne Park footbridge over the river Petteril, 6 December 2015, still passable.

Debris building up against the bridge.
6 December 2015, 12.42 pm.

A helicopter hovers over the flooded Brunton Park football
ground, photographed from Melbourne Park.

Rescue underway at Victoria Road, Botcherby.

Inset: a rescue boat from 2005 on Victoria Road.

The Waverley Viaduct at Engine Lonning gives a good illustration of the quantity of water flowing down the Eden. The water is level with the buttresses supporting the arches. **Inset:** The Waverley viaduct in more clement weather.

Where does the water come from?

This map shows the main rivers feeding into the Eden. All of the water from the catchments of these rivers must pass through the narrow gap between Stanwix Bank on the north side of the river and the Sheepmount on the south bank.